Small Things

Words from my namesake

By

Trude Lisagor

and

Trude Grunwald

Small Things

Words from my namesake

By Trude Lisagor

and Trude Grunwald

ISBN: 1451537069   EAN-13: 9781451537062

Published by: Custom Books Publishing

Printed in the United States of America.

For my grandmother

Contents

Discovery

You were just a portrait on the wall. You looked so much like your daughter—my mother—but in my child's mind, a much fancier version. Pearls around your neck, gold earrings, flowered dress. You tilted your head and made a soft, subtle smile with closed lips. Your eyes, under perfectly arched brows, seemed to hold so much.

Mom shared only a few stories about you. She referred to you as sensitive. Not exactly a compliment coming from her because she valued toughness. She mentioned you liked to write. She implied the move from Germany to Los Angeles was very hard on you—that you had a nervous breakdown. I remember wondering what that meant, but she didn't elaborate. She

1

maintained that when she became a mother herself, you wouldn't babysit because you'd "already raised your own children," as she put it. And, she told me how a drunk driver took your life as you walked on a sidewalk close to home; sometimes she would drive by where it happened to show me. That tragic event happened in the years between my older sister's birth and mine. So, by Jewish tradition, I was named Trude after you.

Even though we were connected through our bloodline and our shared name, you remained just a two-dimensional entity until my early forties when your son, my Uncle Ernie, shared a journal you had written for him that spanned his life from birth to age fifteen. He'd translated it himself from German to English. Mom revealed, for the first time, that she also had a journal that you'd written for her. She explained that many German mothers would secretly record their thoughts and insights about their children and later bestow these treasures as birthday presents when they turned fifteen. She took hers to a German translator, and then I transcribed it and made copies for my sisters and me.

I thought this was so amazing because I had also been keeping a secret journal for both my daughters during their high-school years. It was an idea suggested to me by a colleague at the school where I taught, with the recommendation that I give the journals to them when they graduated. At the time, I had already given my older daughter hers; my younger daughter was still in high school and would have to wait. As I read your beautiful words, you finally came alive for me. I understood how lucky I was to have your name. I felt it wasn't a coincidence or simply a matter of timing; I truly carried you within my life.

Mom passed away in 2009 after a decade of deteriorating health. My sisters and I became closer than ever during that difficult time. It was heartbreaking cleaning her condo and experiencing the physical reminders of the struggles she endured. Her closet held the clothes from her working days still covered in plastic from the cleaners, then stretch pants and tee shirts, and lastly hospital gowns and Depends. We were also surrounded by tangible evidence of what she cherished and gave her joy—art (lithographs by well-known artists mixed with creations by her grandchildren), music, photographs and books.

We found a portfolio hidden in her closet that had a variety of unframed art; for a moment we felt like characters in a movie making a surprising discovery. On the last day of our cleaning, we pulled down some boxes from the den closet. Inside were photographs dating back to the 1920s, my father's high school and college yearbooks (Mom also graduated from Los Angeles High School and UCLA but couldn't afford yearbooks), a chemistry paper that she co-authored and was published in 1953 (who knew?), and then the most amazing thing of all—a worn, striped, cloth-bound journal that we'd never seen or heard of before. We opened to the first page, and it was inscribed in your elegant handwriting:

To Stanley and Lottie on their first Wedding Anniversary, April 3rd, 1948.

The next page was a note to my parents telling them that your gift was short essays you had written some years ago that you wanted to share with them.

We set the journal aside so we could complete our clean up mission with the tantalizing promise of reading it later. Around 11:00 pm and in a state of total exhaustion, we collapsed in the living room and I read your journal aloud from start to finish. We were deeply touched by your words. You wrote in English—perfectly— and we were blown away by your expressive vocabulary, creativity, and lack of spelling or grammatical errors. We were exposed to parts of our family history we had not previously known. The wisdom you had gained from your life experiences leapt from the pages and into our hearts.

I don't know why we were never told about your essays. Were they forgotten? Too private? Painful? Or not something Mom or Dad thought we'd find interesting? There's no one alive to ask now. But, instead of dwelling on these questions, I'd rather share your ideas about life with as many people as possible. In that way, you will live on—not just as a picture on my wall. Yes, my sisters wanted me to have your portrait because I share your name...and now, so much more.

My dear children

My dear children:

These are some of my
little essays which
I composed some years
ago.
I know that they are
not great.
But may the spirit in
which they are thought
and written warm your
hearts! Your loving
Mother.

Small things

If I could share only one of your writings, it would be the essay on Thanksgiving. You wouldn't have even celebrated this American holiday if you hadn't been forced out of your country. Your husband, my grandfather, was a successful Jewish businessman in Germany. He had fought as a German soldier in World War I and had his left leg amputated below the knee because of a battle injury. I remember when the realization hit me in high school that Opa had fought on the German side! Leaving behind your former comfortable life, together you escaped to the United States with your two children. Your expression of appreciation for what you discovered to be most important in life is a lesson for everyone.

Let us give thanks!

(for Thanksgiving Day)

Thanksgiving is a real family feast. All the relatives gather around the splendidly decorated dinner table. The smell of good food raises the spirits. The wine makes everybody feel light and happy, and the abundance of exquisite dishes lets us forget all the worries. I think it is a wonderful idea to celebrate Thanksgiving in this way and I gladly take possession of this ancient custom.

But just now, at the feast of abundance, I want to express my thanks for something—which maybe—you cannot understand: I feel a deep gratitude towards my fate which took from me all the abundance of my former life and made me modest and humble.

In my old country I practically had everything I liked. I certainly felt happy about that, but I took it so much for granted as if it would always stay with me

Then the dreadful happenings befell us. We were forced to leave our old country, a country, beloved by us and our ancestors since centuries. We left, took leave from our old luxury—and a new life began. At first it was a very hard struggle. The new world was rich with disappointments. Nobody knew us. Either we had to help ourselves or we were lost. The first thing was to change mentally. We had to learn how to arrange everything in the most modest way without losing our culture, for living without culture would have been the worst thing for all of us.

But gradually I found out how wonderful life can be without having all my wishes granted, without having abundance of everything. I learned to appreciate the smallest, most unimportant things. And a new *spirit fell upon me: the spirit of being grateful not for the great gifts in life but the very tiny ones. I learned the happiness that goes with everything when it is given with a full heart.*

My sincerest belief and my greatest experience of my new life is: not the abundance makes the life worthy; the real joy goes with the smallest things, when they are given as a genuine sacrifice!

Let me give thanks for my experience which taught me this new attitude towards life.

Get acquainted with yourself

In another essay, you wrote about your thoughts on loneliness. It wasn't the usual interpretation of being lonely rather the idea of taking time to be alone. When I was diagnosed with multiple sclerosis in 1996, I craved and received the support of numerous people—my husband, daughters, mother, sisters, friends, colleagues, doctors, neighbors... I couldn't have made it through without them. Embraced with love, I also discovered that I needed to be able to comfort myself by myself. Up until that time, my life was noisy with my hilarious and loud family, chattering sixth-grade students and our hyper dog. I was busy, busy, busy and loved it. Suddenly my body couldn't and wouldn't keep up. Unable to freely move, I spent many hours alone. Thoughts constantly raced through my mind—some amusing and uplifting, but most depressing and full of fear. This drained much of my limited energy so my therapist suggested I pick a specific time each day to allow these thoughts to run wild. Every morning at 9:30 am I would sit in our upstairs window seat for twenty minutes of obsessive thinking. Then other times when my thoughts turned negative, I would tell myself to wait until my next day's appointment with myself. I learned to quiet my mind and to be alone without being lonely.

Some thoughts about loneliness

Last Monday we read the following quotation which Mrs. Williams had written for us on the blackboard:

"Don't try to flee your loneliness

You'll only find it in the end.

Just get acquainted with yourself,

You'll gain an <u>understanding</u> friend."

I liked this quotation so much that I copied it and that I intend to say some words about this deep thought. I think that nothing in life could be truer than this. Maybe that all of us need a ripe maturity to understand its meaning. Certainly a great philosopher and thinker must have written these words.

As long as we are very young and inexperienced we believe that only distraction and amusement can lead us to our goals. But as time goes on we comprehend that our best thoughts come and the building of ourselves can be accomplished only when we take time to be alone.

I do sincerely hope that each of you, my dear fellow students, has the frequent opportunity to spend a little while alone with yourself. Thus you will discover the true meaning of: "the understanding friend."

I don't want you to get a wrong impression of my married life. But just because I am very happy, I'd like to give you this advice. We all are the same human beings, aroused in joy, downhearted in misfortune. We need a lot of inner strength to balance our emotions for there is hardly a worse thing than to let our *fellowmen suffer from our mood. And in order to win back our balance, we have to be alone. I think that it is the greatest task—especially for us wives and mothers—to be the understanding companion for our loved ones, cheering and soothing whenever the hour demands it. And to gain this self-adjustment, we need to be alone.*

Imagine peace

Until the Vietnam War, my parents and I were a great team. I was a cheerful and agreeable daughter. But as I grew disgruntled with our country's involvement (as many high-school students did), Mom and Dad maintained their faith in our government. Dinner conversations turned into arguments and upset stomachs. I wanted peace, justice, racial equality and, looking back now, I'm sure they did, too. We just had radically different opinions. The war entered our formerly happy home and wreaked havoc.

Added to this poisonous stew was my boyfriend who professed to Mom that he believed in "making love in the streets." She was not pleased at all!

It was a time of marching for peace, rebellion, poetry and leaving home. Forty years later, I'm still married to my hippie love, and we still pray and work for peace. It remains my deepest hope, although it sometimes feels no closer than it did during my teenage years.

Your journal includes a single poem. Its topic is your wish for peace. It reminds me to hang on to our mutual dream and to continue working for its realization. I'm inspired that you could imagine a peaceful world in the midst of your own painful experiences.

A Poem

(composed in World War II)

Thinking of it with joy I beam

Last night I had a wonderful dream:

I walked with delight from place to place,

For I brought peace to the human race.

And everybody shook joyful my hand,

Shouted: "Forever the war has an end,

The hate is over, forgotten the pain,

We are allowed to love again!"

And all the nations, who murdered before

Gathered in peace on paradise shore,

They started singing—a wonderful theme.

--Too bad, the alarm clock ended my dream!

But from the happiness the dream has brought

Remains with vigor the wishful thought

That Peace may come all over the earth

To bring to mankind a purified birth.

Lottie Grunwald Talpis

(My mother as a child in Germany)

Indelible influences

The first essay in your journal is about your own grandmother and how she, more than anyone, influenced your life. My sisters and I had not heard stories about her before. We also didn't know that your brother was killed in World War I. Your grandmother lived with your family during your childhood and, through her example, gave you the tools to surmount the challenges that awaited you.

I flew to Los Angeles during what turned out to be the last week of Mom's life. Her doctor had sent her to the hospital for tests because she was complaining about pain that seemed different from what she usually experienced. She'd been in and out of the hospital many times and, despite her years of poor health, always managed to rally back. When I walked into the room, her first words were, "Did you come to say good bye?" She'd delivered the same cutting question on a visit I made a year earlier and, again, she caught me off guard. Her motto was "love is never having to say I love you," whereas in my house, we freely and frequently exchanged those three little words. Her grandchildren had softened her over the years, but whenever she uttered, "I love you," it was with a twinkle in her eye.

This powerhouse of a woman looked incredibly frail and uncomfortable. She was terribly nauseous, so I held a tray near her mouth and gently wiped her lips. Still, we managed to have conversations and moments that were filled with laughter, depth and love. At one point, I needed the nurses to help her back into bed because she was blacking out in her wheelchair. When they asked her to lift her head for the pillow, in her weakened state, she managed to flip them the bird with a mischievous smile.

She couldn't believe how her arm and hand shook when she tried to eat. And, she didn't want to discuss the diagnosis she had just received—cancer that had started in her lungs and spread throughout her body. Her cigarette smoking had been her pleasure and her fuck-you to the world—at 83, she'd already outlived my father, her brother and the ages at which her own parents had passed. But Mom had come to her decision about the course of her treatment and told her doctor she didn't want any more.

That night in bed, as I reflected on the tremendous amount of angst I'd experienced over our 57-year relationship, I thought about what I wanted to say to her the next day if I had the chance. I knew it would have to be succinct and not overly mushy. By the time I got up in the morning, I'd figured it out.

I drove to the hospital early to meet with the hospice nurse. After she explained the alternatives and left the room, Mom asked me what I thought she should do next. I gave my opinion and realized it was the perfect opportunity to express my feelings.

Looking directly in her eyes, I said, "Of all the people in my life, you've influenced me the most."

She whispered, "Thank you," as a tear slipped out and rolled down her cheek.

I continued, "I know we have different personalities, but we also have a lot in common. We're both strong and tough and generous."

She nodded in agreement.

Then, most important, I affirmed, "I love you very much."

She responded, "You definitely made up for all the diapers I changed!"

Your description and love for your grandma show how we're often most influenced by people whose names won't be found in history books. It reminds me that the manner in which I live my life truly matters.

My Most Unforgettable Character

When I speak about my most unforgettable character I see my little grandma so distinctly before my inward eye as if she were sitting among us. She was a very small woman with a light complexion and deep blue eyes. She always had a little smile on her lips and this was the expression of her soul. She lived in my parents' home from my very first days and I cannot think of my childhood without knowing her around us. But as a youngster I never would have recognized the deep influence she brought into my life.

My grandmother was the wisest human being I ever met—and probably—I shall meet. She taught me how to see the world. She had a good word for everyone for she tried to see the worthy deeds of everybody and to overlook his faults. And by doing this she gave to each individual, who was lucky enough to meet her, an enrichment of himself, either by encouraging him or by comforting him or—if necessary—by making him modest and natural.

She was very religious and believed in Providence. She thought that each fate—even the hardest—had its good sides. I will never forget the day on which we got the message that my brother had been killed in World War I. My brother had been the whole pride of my grandmother; it was her only grandson besides having four granddaughters. My parents were on a trip and I was quite alone with my grandma. It was my first big loss in my young life and I could not refrain from crying bitterly. When she saw me so desperate she touched my shoulder and asked me not to grumble. She told me that it was a much greater mercy to know my brother dead than to see him coming back either blind or without hearing, especially as he intended to become a musician. I could not see any comfort in her words but in later years I learned that she was right.

She died as happily as she had lived. One morning she woke me up and told me that she would go home today. After two hours, she had succumbed, bearing the same happy smile on her lips as she had always shown during her life. Her wish had been fulfilled; she had gone home as peacefully as she had lived.

To me this event will never be forgotten. I felt the majesty, the grandeur and the happiness that even Death can bring to a human being when it has accomplished a blessed and wonderful life.

My mother and father

1985

Real genius

I love how you transition from your reflections on an extremely personal heroine, your grandmother, to writing about a newfound hero, Abraham Lincoln. You mention his humility and compassion—traits I would also attribute to you.

Your thoughts on Lincoln were fresh and insightful. I think your own experiences caused you to recognize and understand more than most about this great man. In spite—or because—of his difficult life, he managed to accomplish so much. His struggles were a testament to the good that can arise from extreme pain, weakness or even past mistakes.

Rather than allowing our own hardships and obstacles to stop us from fulfilling our goals, you show that we must use them as fodder for creating a better world. This is a recurring theme in your life and inspires me to do the same.

Some words about Abraham Lincoln's shyness and modesty from the psychological standpoint

Abraham Lincoln was brought up in very poor surroundings. He accomplished his education by picking up literary crumbs here and there. His married life was not very happy. He was awkward and shy in his manners. And yet, he was elected President of the United States. He became President not on account of his own ambition. The people of his time recognized the genius in him.

When we look over the history of mankind we always find that a real genius never is satisfied with the deeds he performs. He studies and struggles to penetrate the secrets of the universe. By listening to the wonderful music of Beethoven, Mozart or Schubert we hardly realize that this eternal music was composed in bitter need and in a desperate mood. But the inspiration came in spite of mental depression and lack of comfort. All the thoughts, wishes and dreams were brought into music, and this music was the revelation of the soul. I just read a book about the Life of Tchaikovsky. Out of his deepest depression and contempt of himself was born his greatest work which will stand for all eternity: his Sixth Symphony.

And now back to Lincoln. Was he not a genius as great as all these musicians? Did he not strive for the highest rights of humanity: for Liberty for All? Would he have been so full of understanding if he had not gone through need and misery himself? I think that he felt the wants and desires of his people—even of the slaves—so deeply, because he himself had to struggle so bitterly.

A real genius cannot be formed by surroundings and education. This genuineness comes from within. And for this reason Lincoln could not be otherwise than *modest and even shy. He was humbly devoted to one task: to free humanity from slavery and oppression. He considered himself only as an interpreter to attain the goal. And as long as he had not reached the realization of his ideals he remained a seeker and a stumbler. These are my ideas about the shyness and modesty of a great genius: Abraham Lincoln.*

The art of giving

Your closing thoughts touch on the art of giving from the heart and not for recognition. Your parents set a wonderful example, and you passed this on to your children. The family members who followed have continued your generosity.

Epilogue

Experience in life has taught me never to estimate people by their words but by their deeds. I was reared in a home where this experience was a reality. My parents had the pure art of life never to boast of their good deeds but to be charitable in the most modest way.

My grandma had been the founder of the Red Cross in our little hometown. My mother became her successor and worked so successfully that she was given two decorations: the Red Cross and the Queen Louise Order. I don't tell it to be obtrusive, but only to show how charity and humanity should be practiced. My parents spent a lot of their time and money in helping others. They did it so secretly that even we children did not know whom they supplied. I can hardly remember a single day at home without seeing big kettles with food on the oven. These kettles were taken away every noon to feed undernourished families or to strengthen mothers who had just given birth to a child.

This impression grew so deep within me that I never could and never will understand how men can give in a loud and public way. I think that real charity should be done from heart to heart. It is not only the money and the material things which help to comfort our poor ones, but it is also the way that these things are given.

The best lesson I received in my youth was the art of giving. I did a lot of social work myself in my later years—and still am doing—and I always tried and shall try to practice what I have seen at home.

It is my holy task to educate my children in the same way, that they may be worthy of their ancestors.

Closing thoughts

I hold your journal in my hands, gathering these closing thoughts. I can sense your DNA embedded in the faded cloth cover. It seems, for a moment, that I could reach across time to touch you.

Now that I'm also a Grandma Trude, I'm determined to share your realizations about life with even more generations. I'm so grateful to have discovered your writing. It just shows that we don't know how our words might influence the future.

Regardless of our place in history, there are several basic truths that endure. As you shared in your essays, we should take time to self-reflect and to express appreciation. The art of giving is as essential as the dream of peace. And we must value life's struggles while realizing how others influence our lives.

How amazing that this small discovery, tucked among the boxes in my mother's closet for sixty years, would have such a profound impact.

With appreciation to...

My parents, Lottie and Stan, for hanging on to my grandmother's essays through the many stages, ages and moves in their lifetimes.

My sisters, Carol and Peggy, for their love, laughter and lifelong friendship.

My daughters, Megan and Jamie, for simply everything.

Terri, Lynne, Nina, Tim, Joanne, Nancy, Mary Lou, Linda and Marilyn for reviews and encouragement.

And, of course, my hippie love, Mike, who helped me every step of the way.

Please visit: www.voiceseducation.org

Made in the USA
Charleston, SC
12 August 2010